This book belongs to:

_____

_____

Shade squares in the grid to create your name in pixel text.

THIS IS NOT A MATH BOOK

Kane Miller
A DIVISION OF EDC PUBLISHING

First American Edition 2015
Kane Miller, A Division of EDC Publishing

Copyright © 2015 Ivy Press Limited

For information contact:
Kane Miller, A Divison of EDC Publishing
PO Box 470663
Tulsa, OK 74147-0663
www.kanemiller.com
www.edcpub.com
www.usbornebooksandmore.com

Library of Congress Control Number: 2014943088

Printed in China

3 4 5 6 7 8 9 10

ISBN: 978-1-61067-358-7

Image credit: (pages 7 and 31) © CC-BY-SA 2.5 Thomas Steiner
(page 87) © Rodin Anton/Shutterstock.com

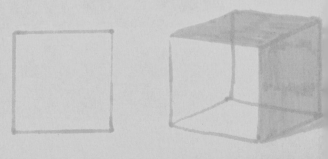

CONTENTS

Math and Art ...

AT FIRST GLANCE, THEY MIGHT
SEEM TO BE WORLDS APART.

But look a little closer
and you'll see that they
have a lot in common.

MATH IS FULL OF **PATTERNS**,

AND PATTERNS CAN BE beautiful,
decorative and complex.

Did you know that our brains are tuned in to pattern and rhythm, which are really big parts of both math and art? With a touch of creativity, art can bring numbers and shapes to life. And then amazing things can happen! A series of numbers can create awesome spiral shapes (pages 50-53), or a series of points on an axis can make an intricate 3-D web (pages 18-19). Mathematical principles allow us to draw in perspective (pages 60-63) and create incredible illusions (pages 64-65), while mathematical puzzles (pages 34-35) can boggle the brain and make art.

The activities in this book will not only help you to see how math and art connect, but they are also fun to do!

Once you know how to do an activity, you can create your own artworks on the pages. Don't forget to use the blank paper and graph paper at the back of the book for practice, or for trying out your own awesome art ideas.

YOUR TOOLBOX

YOU ONLY NEED A FEW THINGS TO MAKE SMART MATH ART: PAPER, A PENCIL AND A RULER. BUT A FEW EXTRA TOOLS WILL HELP YOU TAKE YOUR ART TO THE NEXT LEVEL.

PROTRACTOR: use this to draw angles. One edge is flat but the other edge is curved to form half a circle and is marked with degrees—the unit of measurement used to describe angles—from 0° to 180°.

ANGLES: if you don't have a protractor, you can still do all of the activities that require one by using these angle pieces. Trace them, cut them out and use them whenever you need an angle!

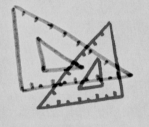

60°

72°

36°

45°

30°

90°

COMPASS: this tool is essential for drawing perfect circles. It looks like a V. On one leg of the V is a pencil, and on the other leg is a spike. You press the spike into your paper, so that you can swing the pencil around a central point. Learn how to use a compass on page 11.

TAPE: ordinary adhesive tape is all you need.

GRAPH PAPER: this is paper marked with a square or triangular grid. You'll find some graph paper at the back of this book.

PLAIN PAPER: use plain paper for drawing or for projects where you want to cut out shapes. You'll find some plain pages at the back of this book.

TRACING PAPER: sometimes you'll be asked to trace shapes. You can use the plain paper at the back of this book.

SCISSORS: sometimes you'll be asked to cut out shapes, like the angles, opposite. Use a small pair of scissors.

Perfect
CIRCLES

How perfect is your circle?
Try to draw freehand
circles—make them as
perfect as you can.

Fill this space with overlapping circles!

TRY IT!

Color your overlapping circles so every section is next to a different color.

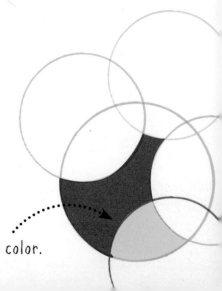

CIRCLE CHALLENGE!

TRY DRAWING A CIRCLE THROUGH THREE POINTS. DID YOU KNOW THAT YOU CAN DRAW ONLY ONE CIRCLE THROUGH ANY PARTICULAR GROUP OF THREE POINTS?

Can you draw a circle through these three points?

ANOTHER CHALLENGE!

USE YOUR COMPASS TO DRAW A PERFECT CIRCLE.

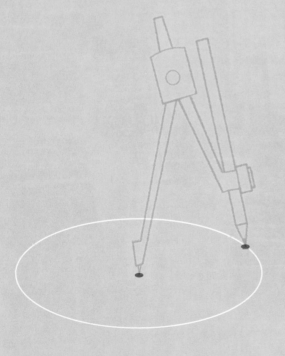

1
PLACE THE POINT OF THE COMPASS HERE.
This is the circle's center.

2
PLACE THE PENCIL HERE.
The distance between this point and the center is called the radius.

3
Now, spin the pencil around the point of the compass to draw a perfect circle.

CIRCULATE

DON'T UNDERESTIMATE THE CIRCLE! YOU CAN MAKE
SOME AMAZING SHAPES IF YOU LINK AND OVERLAP
YOUR CIRCLES. SEE WHAT PATTERNS YOU CAN MAKE.

1 Place the compass point where two grid lines intersect (cross each other).

2 Draw a circle that takes up four squares.

3 Keep going!

4 Color in the petals.

Use your compass and a square grid.
Like these petals? Look in the back of the book for more graph paper to draw some more!

PRETTY PETALS

1 Place the compass point at every intersection.

2 Draw a circle that surrounds six triangles.

3 Fill the grid with circles.

4 Color in the petal shapes.

Use your compass and a triangular grid.

Circle LOOOOOOOVE

IS IT A HEART? AN APPLE? A PINECONE? IT'S UP TO YOU! THIS SHAPE, MADE
FROM OVERLAPPING CIRCLES, IS CALLED A CARDIOID. THE CARDIOID PART IS
ACTUALLY JUST THE OUTER EDGE, BUT THE CIRCLES ON THE INSIDE LOOK AWESOME.

Try coloring it in. The checkered pattern looks cooool!

create a cardioid!

FOLLOWING THE STEPS AT THE BOTTOM OF THE PAGE, USE THE NUMBERED CIRCLE, BELOW, TO PRACTICE. THEN USE SOME PLAIN PAPER TO DRAW YOUR OWN.

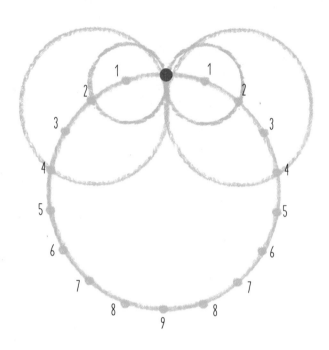

top

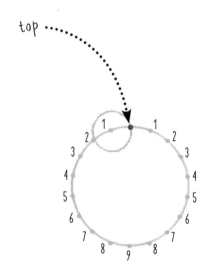

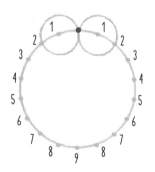

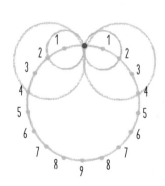

1 Using a compass, draw a circle with the center at point 1. The circle should go through the TOP point.

2 Draw another circle beside it with its center at the other point 1. Make sure it passes through the TOP.

3 Draw two larger circles centered at points 2, then repeat until point 9. Finish with a single circle—your largest!

Diabolic PARABOLIC

You don't need circles to make curves. You can make curves from straight lines!
Try this and see. Continue the pattern below using a ruler to draw straight
lines to connect matching numbers (1 to 1, 2 to 2 and so on).

The type of curve
you're making is called a

PARABOLIC
CURVE

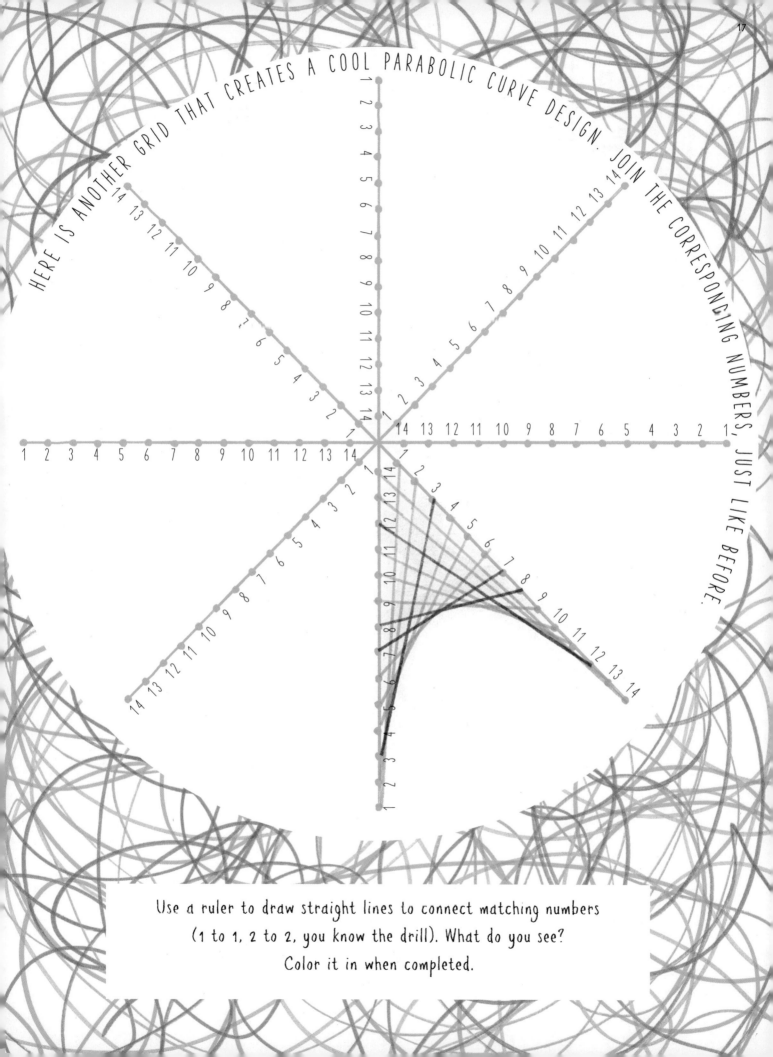

HERE IS ANOTHER GRID THAT CREATES A COOL PARABOLIC CURVE DESIGN. JOIN THE CORRESPONDING NUMBERS, JUST LIKE BEFORE.

Use a ruler to draw straight lines to connect matching numbers
(1 to 1, 2 to 2, you know the drill). What do you see?
Color it in when completed.

Wonder
WEBS

Overlap **parabolic curves** and create a web that would make a spider proud!

CONNECT CORRESPONDING NUMBERS AROUND THE TRIANGLE. RED TO BLUE, BLUE TO GREEN AND GREEN TO RED.

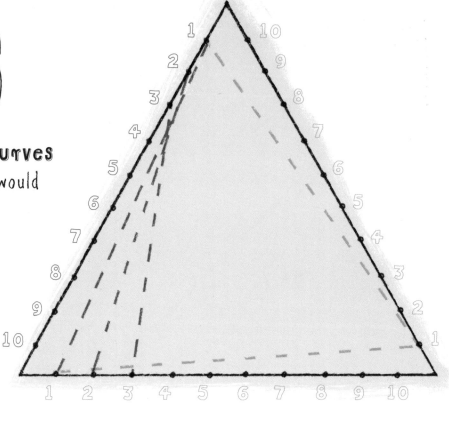

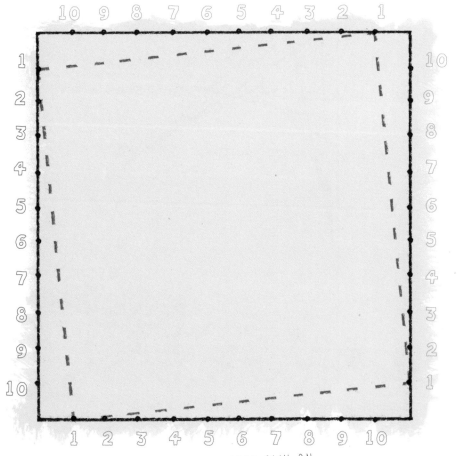

Now try a square. Connect red to gray, gray to green, green to blue and blue to red.

WHAT WEBS CAN YOU WEAVE? TRY YOUR OWN ON THE BLANK PAPER AT THE BACK OF THE BOOK.

FIND THE MYSTERY CURVE MADE BY CONNECTING POINTS ON A CIRCLE.

Join each RED number to its double, 1 to 2, 2 to 4, 3 to 6... Then do exactly the same with the GREEN numbers. When you connect 18 to 36, you're done.

WHAT SHAPE APPEARS AS YOU DRAW THE LINES?
CAN YOU FIND THIS SAME SHAPE SOMEWHERE ELSE IN THIS BOOK?

Find the answer on page 14.

Infinite CIRCLES

Did you know that you can fit an infinite number of circles in a finite space? What's the largest circle you can fit in this triangle? Fill the spaces that are left with the biggest circles you can.

Circles can snuggle into the smallest spaces.

HOW MANY CIRCLES CAN YOU SQUEEZE IN?

DRAW THE LARGEST CIRCLE YOU CAN IN EACH TRIANGLE.

Then snuggle circles into the remaining spaces. Always draw the largest circle you can.

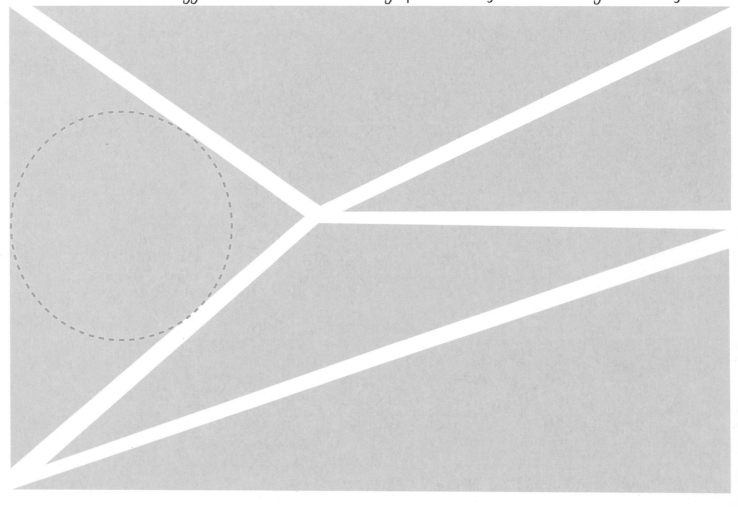

LIKE BUBBLES FILLING A BUBBLE WAND, FILL THIS CIRCLE WITH CIRCLES.

THIS DRAWING STARTED WITH A GIANT OUTER CIRCLE CONTAINING A SMALLER CIRCLE EXACTLY HALF ITS HEIGHT. CONTINUE THE DRAWING BY MAKING ANOTHER HALF-SIZED CIRCLE BELOW THE FIRST ONE. FILL IN THE REMAINING SPACE. TRY IT FREEHAND.

MANDALAS

A MANDALA IS A SYMBOLIC PATTERN THAT REPRESENTS THE UNIVERSE. USE THE TECHNIQUES YOU'VE WORKED WITH SO FAR TO CREATE ONE.

1

6   14

11   9

16   4

13   17

18   12

3   7

8   2

5   15

10

USE A RULER TO CONNECT THE DOTS AROUND THE CIRCLE IN ORDER: 1 TO 2, 2 TO 3 AND SO ON. WHEN YOU GET TO 18, CONNECT IT BACK TO 1.

Fill in the spaces with colors, circles, parabolic curves or flowers!

COMPLEX BUT AWESOME!

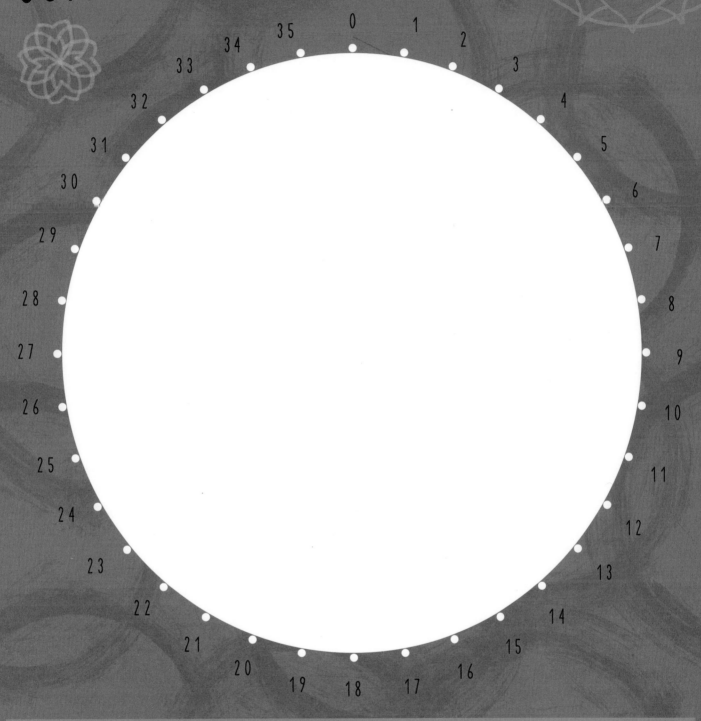

1 Start at 0. Connect every fifth dot. When you reach 35, count forward five numbers to 4. When you reach 34, count forward five numbers to 3. Keep going in fives until you return to 0.

2 Starting at 0 again, connect every eleventh dot. When you reach 33, count forward eleven dots to 8. Keep going in elevens until you return to 0.

3 Start at 0! Connect every fifteenth dot, just like before. When you get to 0, connect every nineteenth dot. When you get back to 0, your pattern is complete!

Let's try TRIANGLES

To make a triangle, you first need to connect three points.
Practice drawing a right triangle using the steps below,
and then use it to make beautiful patterns.

THE RIGHT TRIANGLE has a 90° angle in one corner.

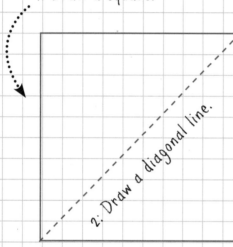

1: Draw a square.

2: Draw a diagonal line.

3: Erase one of the halves.

90°

Tile-angles

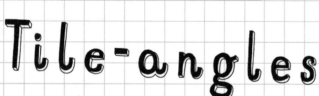

USE TINY TRIANGLES TO MAKE BEAUTIFUL PATTERNS.

Color in half of a grid square triangle-style.

Now you have two triangles, one white and one red.

Put your triangle tiles next to each other to make a larger pattern.

Keep the pattern going...

CONTINUE THESE TILE-ANGLE PATTERNS!

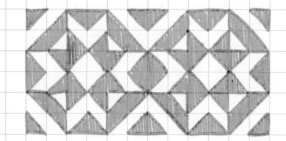

Now you try! Use the
graph paper at the back
of the book to make your
own tile-angle patterns.

A tricky triangle!

AN EQUILATERAL TRIANGLE's three sides are the same length.
There are two ways to draw it. Try them both!

ANGLE METHOD:

1: Use the 60° angle piece from page 8.

2: Use a ruler to draw two sides—make sure they are the same length.

3: Connect the ends of the two sides to make a third side. This side should be the same length as the other two.

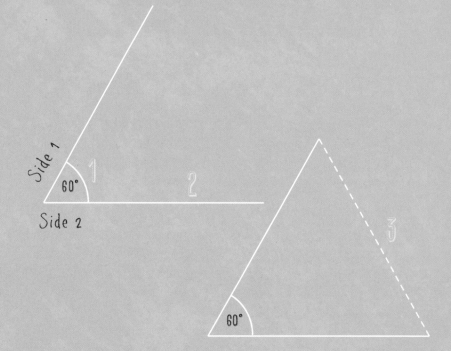

Side 1

1

2

60°

Side 2

3

60°

NOW DRAW ONE OF YOUR OWN!

COMPASS METHOD:

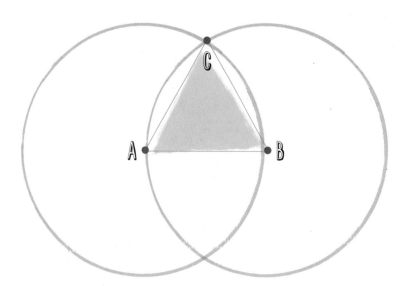

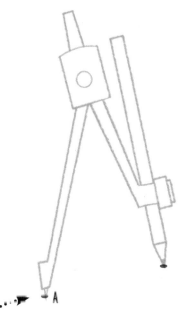

1 Set your compass to the length you want the sides of the equilateral triangle to be.

2 Use your compass to draw a circle and mark the center with a dot—dot A.

3 Draw a dot (B) on the circle. Place your compass point at B and draw a circle, but make sure this circle passes through A.

4 Find the spot where the two circles cross, and draw dot C. Use your ruler and connect the dots to form an equilateral triangle!

NOW DRAW ONE OF YOUR OWN!

Feeling Fractal

IN A FRACTAL PATTERN, THE SAME IMAGE IS REPEATED SMALLER AND SMALLER AND SMALLER, FOREVER AND EVER. YOU CAN ZOOM IN ON ANY PART OF IT AND IT WILL LOOK EXACTLY THE SAME AS IT DID ZOOMED OUT. YOU CAN KEEP ZOOMING IN FOREVER AND THE PATTERN WILL STILL BE REPEATED ALL THE WAY DOWN.

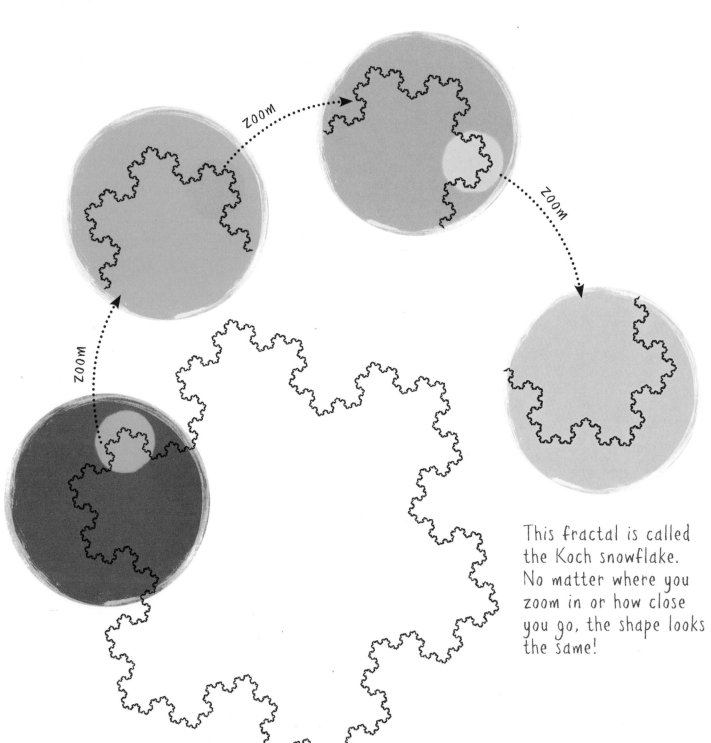

ZOOM

ZOOM

ZOOM

This fractal is called the Koch snowflake. No matter where you zoom in or how close you go, the shape looks the same!

CREATE A KOCH SNOWFLAKE

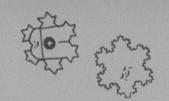

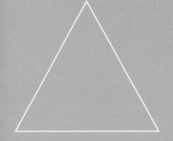

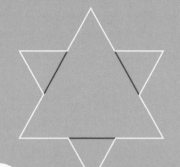

1 Draw an equilateral triangle (see page 27). Using the 60° angle from page 8 will help you.

2 Add smaller triangles on the sides of the first triangle to make a six-pointed star.

3 Draw an even smaller triangle in the middle of each side of each triangle.

4 Keep adding triangles in the middle of each side of each triangle. Fractals never end!

CREATE A FRACTAL!

TRY AN UN-FLAKY FRACTAL—
THE SIERPINSKI TRIANGLE

1 Draw a big triangle, pointing up.

2 Draw an upside-down triangle inside the big triangle, with the corners touching the mid-points of the big triangle's edges.

3 Draw upside-down triangles inside every right-side up triangle, until you can't draw any smaller!

IT'S COOL TO DRAW ONE!

CAN'T GET ENOUGH SIERPINSKI? USE THE TRIANGLE GRAPH PAPER AT THE BACK OF THE BOOK TO DRAW MORE.

Try Sierpinstrees

These Sierpinski triangles look like little trees. Add your own in the spaces and color them. Now add a few Koch snowflakes to create a math forest in a blizzard!

WHY NOT COLOR THE UPSIDE-DOWN AND RIGHT-SIDE UP TRIANGLES DIFFERENT COLORS?

Pascal's Patterns

Let's make triangles with numbers!

Pascal's Triangle always starts with a number 1 at the top. The next row has two more 1s.

After that, each number is the sum of the two numbers above it. Except for the edges, which are always 1s.

Now fill in the rest!

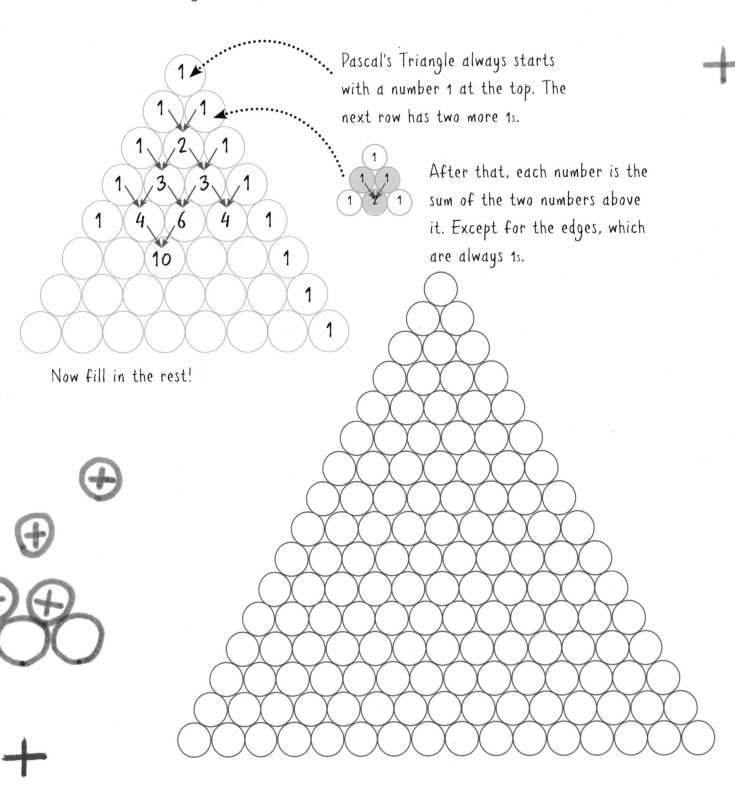

COLOR THE EVEN NUMBERS ONE COLOR AND THE ODD NUMBERS ANOTHER. SEE WHAT HAPPENS. DOES THE PATTERN THAT APPEARS LOOK FAMILIAR?

Make a Pascal's Triangle

THIS TRIANGLE IS FILLED IN FOR YOU.
TRY COLORING IN MULTIPLES OF 4 AND 6
AND SEE THE PATTERNS EMERGE.

For multiples of 6,
color up to row 17.

For multiples
of 4, color
up to row 24.

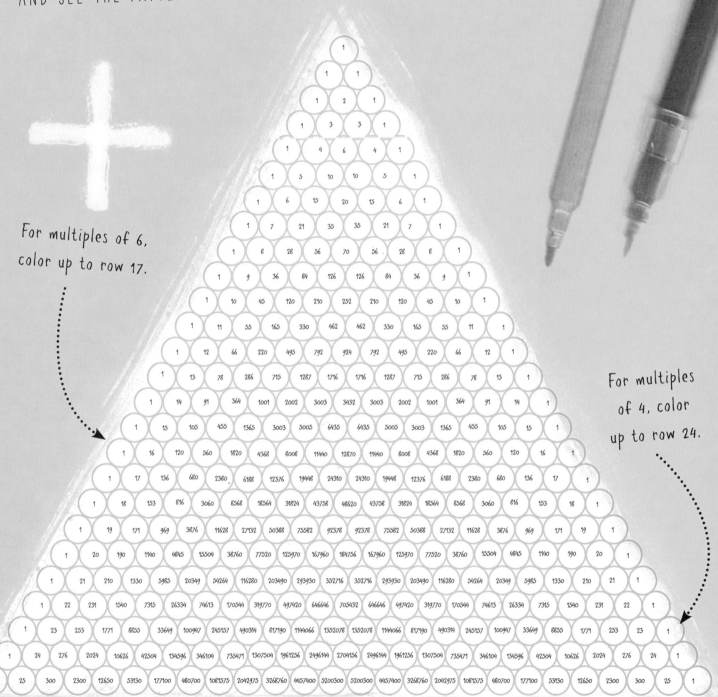

STOMACHION

THE STOMACHION IS A FUN PUZZLE THAT WAS INVENTED THOUSANDS OF YEARS AGO. TO SOLVE THE PUZZLE, YOU FIT 14 DIFFERENT SHAPES TOGETHER TO MAKE FUN IMAGES LIKE ANIMALS OR PLANTS.

THESE ARE THE 14 SHAPES THAT MAKE UP THE STOMACHION:

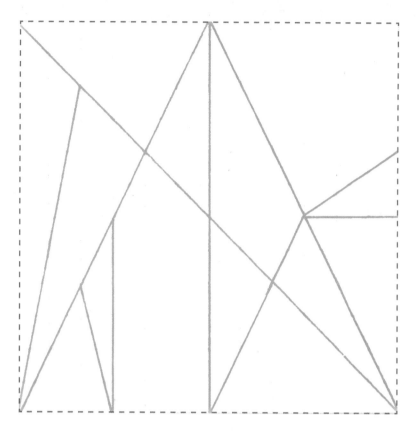

Trace these shapes onto a piece of paper and cut out. See if you can fit them into the blue elephant and the red robot.

MAKE A STOMACHION PUZZLE

Arrange the cut pieces into any shape you like in the space below. Then trace around the outside of your shape. Decorate your shape. Puzzle complete!

FIT THE STOMACHION PIECES INTO
THE SQUARE OR THE TRIANGLE IN AS
MANY DIFFERENT WAYS AS YOU CAN!

Perfect your HEXAGONS

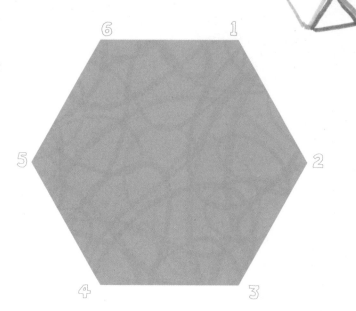

A hexagon has six sides and six angles. In a perfect hexagon, all the sides and angles are exactly the same. There are two ways to make a perfect hexagon:

TRIANGLE METHOD

1: Draw an equilateral triangle. (Check out page 27 to learn how.)

2: Make a second equilateral triangle that shares one side with the first.

3: Make a third equilateral triangle that shares one side with the second.

4: Draw three more equilateral triangles below the first three.

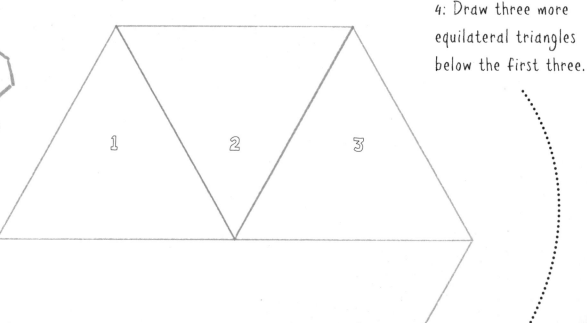

CIRCLE METHOD

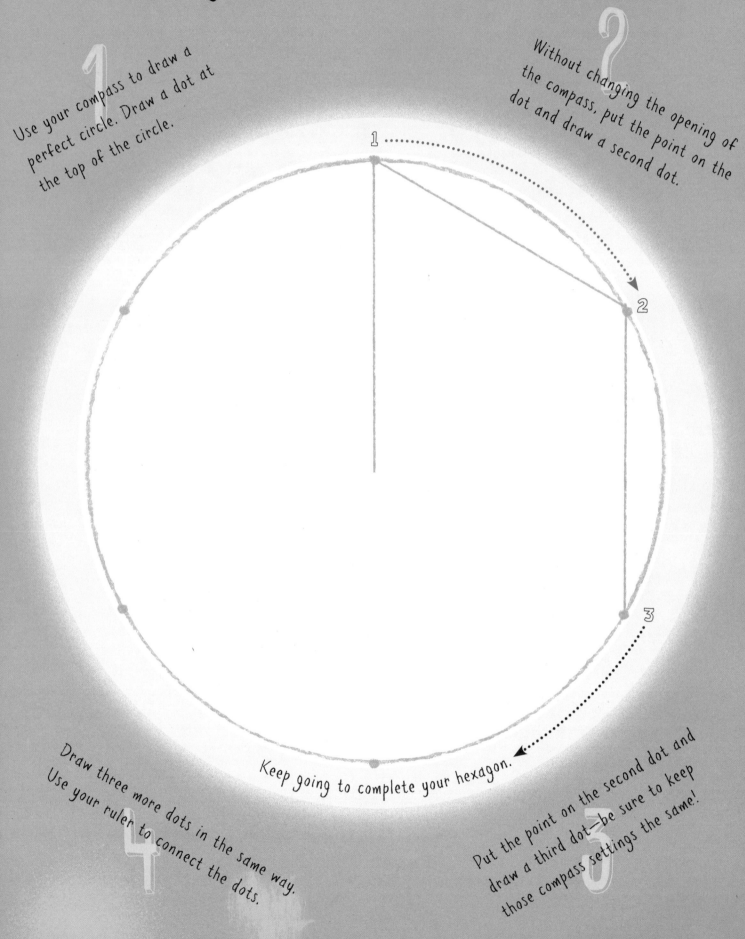

1 Use your compass to draw a perfect circle. Draw a dot at the top of the circle.

2 Without changing the opening of the compass, put the point on the dot and draw a second dot.

3 Put the point on the second dot and draw a third dot—be sure to keep those compass settings the same!

Keep going to complete your hexagon.

4 Draw three more dots in the same way. Use your ruler to connect the dots.

TESSELLATION CREATIONS

A tessellation is a pattern made by repeating shapes. It's great to tessellate! Just cover a flat surface with a pattern of shapes with no gaps or overlays. Complete these tessellations, using a ruler and the angle pieces or a protractor.

TRIANGLES+HEXAGONS   Keep it going!

Make up your own tessellation! Use the plain paper at the end of this book.

SQUARES + TRIANGLES   Keep it going.

Keep it going!

SQUARES + TRIANGLES + HEXAGONS

TRANSFORMERS

Tessellations don't have to be made from perfect shapes. Puzzle pieces aren't squares—and they tessellate! Cut and tape to turn a square into your own tessellation puzzle piece.

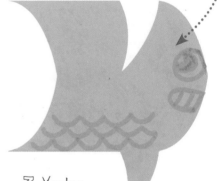

Decorate them however you like.

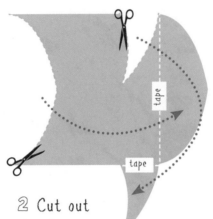

1 Trace and cut out this square from a blank piece of paper. Draw on the lines.

2 Cut out the shapes. Slide these pieces to the opposite side of the square and tape them!

3 You've made your puzzle piece! Trace around it to start your tessellation.

CONTINUE THE PATTERN!

TRACE AROUND YOUR PUZZLE PIECE AND TRY TO COVER THE WHOLE PAGE WITH YOUR TESSELLATION.

TRY THIS!

Cut and tape to create a puzzle piece as before, then trace it to continue the pattern.

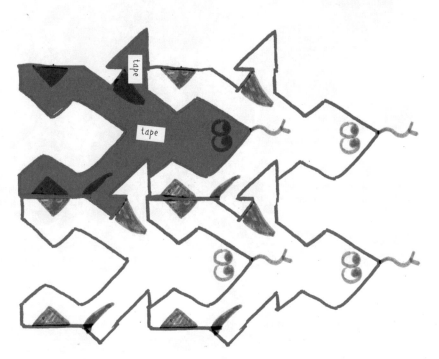

USE THE BLANK PAPER AT THE BACK OF THE BOOK TO DESIGN AND CUT OUT YOUR OWN TESSELLATION PIECE. THEN, TRACE IT HERE!

shape shifters

Tip: start with simple shapes...

Continue with this design or make one of your own.

See how the shapes change as they move across the page? Start off with a simple tessellation and gradually change it into something different!

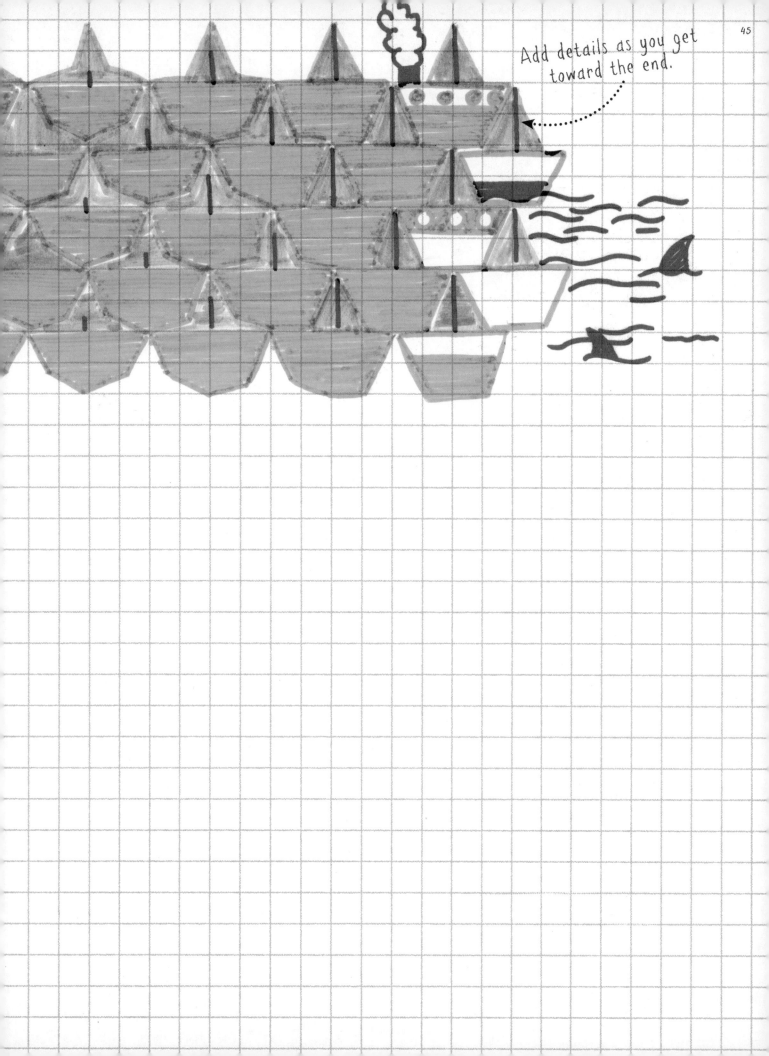

Add details as you get toward the end.

SEAL SPIN!

NOW MAKE A TESSELLATION THAT SPINS!

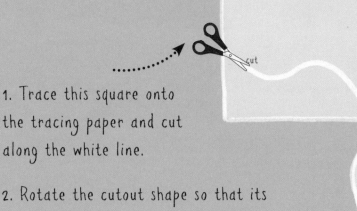

1. Trace this square onto the tracing paper and cut along the white line.

2. Rotate the cutout shape so that its flat edge lines up with the left edge of the square. Tape it in place.

3. Sketch this shape along the top edge and cut out.

4. Rotate your new cutout piece so that its flat edge lines up with the right-hand edge of the square. Tape it in place!

5. Your puzzle piece is now ready to trace around and tessellate. Add smiley seal faces as you go!

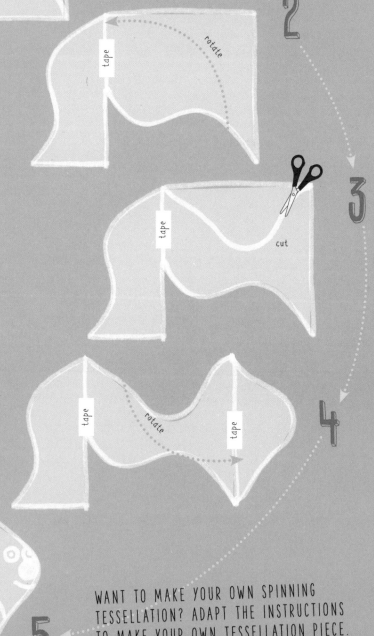

WANT TO MAKE YOUR OWN SPINNING TESSELLATION? ADAPT THE INSTRUCTIONS TO MAKE YOUR OWN TESSELLATION PIECE. USE THE PAPER AT THE BACK OF THE BOOK TO CUT OUT AND TRACE YOUR TESSELLATION!

COVER THE PAGE IN SEALS!

48

PAINTING BY NUMBERS

1	2	3	4	5	6	7	8	9	10
11	12	13	14	15	16	17	18	19	20
21	22	23	24	25	26	27	28	29	30
31	32	33	34	35	36	37	38	39	40
41	42	43	44	45	46	47	48	49	50
51	52	53	54	55	56	57	58	59	60
61	62	63	64	65	66	67	68	69	70
71	72	73	74	75	76	77	78	79	80
81	82	83	84	85	86	87	88	89	90
91	92	93	94	95	96	97	98	99	100

When you arrange numbers into grids, they make patterns. See how the multiples of 2 come in vertical stripes, and the multiples of 3 make diagonal stripes? Now try coloring in multiples of 4.

The patterns get crazier when you color in multiples of 7, 9 or 11. Try different multiples and see what you can make!

1	2	3	4	5	6	7	8	9	10
11	12	13	14	15	16	17	18	19	20
21	22	23	24	25	26	27	28	29	30
31	32	33	34	35	36	37	38	39	40
41	42	43	44	45	46	47	48	49	50
51	52	53	54	55	56	57	58	59	60
61	62	63	64	65	66	67	68	69	70
71	72	73	74	75	76	77	78	79	80
81	82	83	84	85	86	87	88	89	90
91	92	93	94	95	96	97	98	99	100

ROWS OF 9

1	2	3	4	5	6	7	8	9
10	11	12	13	14	15	16	17	18
19	20	21	22	23	24	25	26	27
28	29	30	31	32	33	34	35	36
37	38	39	40	41	42	43	44	45
46	47	48	49	50	51	52	53	54
55	56	57	58	59	60	61	62	63
64	65	66	67	68	69	70	71	72
73	74	75	76	77	78	79	80	81

ROWS OF 7

1	2	3	4	5	6	7
8	9	10	11	12	13	14
15	16	17	18	19	20	21
22	23	24	25	26	27	28
29	30	31	32	33	34	35
36	37	38	39	40	41	42
43	44	45	46	47	48	49

1	2	3	4	5	6	7	8	9	10	11	12
13	14	15	16	17	18	19	20	21	22	23	24
25	26	27	28	29	30	31	32	33	34	35	36
37	38	39	40	41	42	43	44	45	46	47	48
49	50	51	52	53	54	55	56	57	58	59	60
61	62	63	64	65	66	67	68	69	70	71	72
73	74	75	76	77	78	79	80	81	82	83	84
85	86	87	88	89	90	91	92	93	94	95	96
97	98	99	100	101	102	103	104	105	106	107	108
109	110	111	112	113	114	115	116	117	118	119	120
121	122	123	124	125	126	127	128	129	130	131	132
133	134	135	136	137	138	139	140	141	142	143	144

ROWS OF 12

The patterns get even better when you use grids of different sizes. Try coloring in multiples in these grids arranged in rows of 7, 9 and 12. Do you always get the same pattern when you color multiples of 2? What about other multiples?

Loop-de-Loops

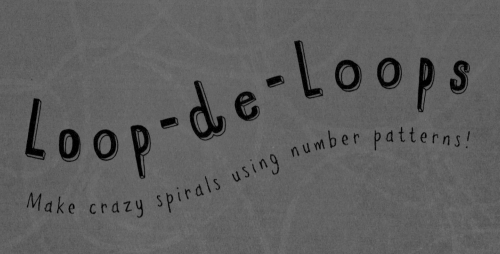

Make crazy spirals using number patterns!

1 FIRST, PICK THREE NUMBERS. HOW ABOUT 2, 3 AND 4?

2 PICK A POINT ON THE GRID TO START.

3 START DRAWING LINES IN A SPIRAL (FIRST TO THE RIGHT, THEN UP, THEN TO THE LEFT, AND THEN DOWN). MAKE YOUR FIRST LINE 2 SQUARES LONG, NEXT 3 SQUARES LONG, NEXT 4 SQUARES LONG, AND THEN GO BACK TO 2 SQUARES LONG FOR THE DOWN STROKE.

4 KEEP DRAWING AROUND AND AROUND UNTIL YOU GET BACK TO THE START! YOU'VE MADE A 2-3-4 LOOP-DE-LOOP!

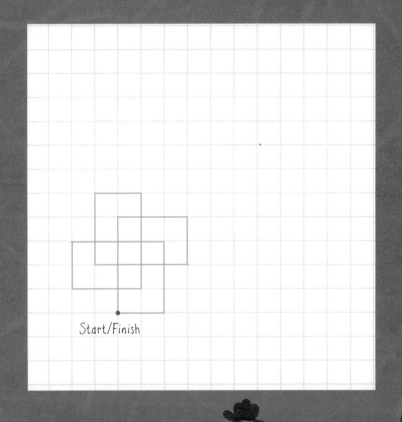

Start/Finish

YOU CAN COLOR YOUR LOOP-DE-LOOP WHEN IT'S DONE.

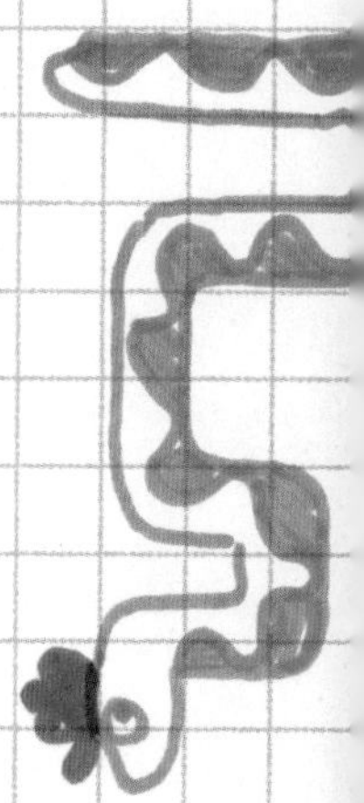

MAKE A 2-1-4 LOOP-DE-LOOP.

MAKE A 3-5-2 LOOP-DE-LOOP!
(Don't worry if some of the lines overlap.)

Start/Finish

Start/Finish

WHAT DO YOU THINK WOULD HAPPEN IF YOU SWITCHED 2-1-4 TO 4-1-2? TRY IT!

Now make your own!

How about some color?

Let's go LOOP-DE-LOOPY!

Loop-de-Loops don't have to use only three numbers...

What does a 5-4-3-2 Loop-de-Loop look like?

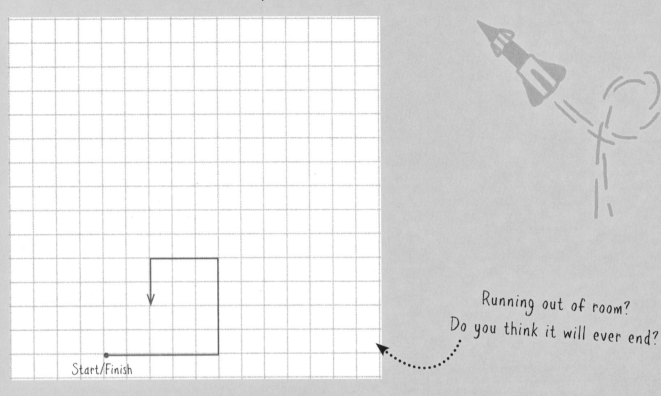

Start/Finish

Running out of room?
Do you think it will ever end?

How about a 1-2-3-4-5
Loop-de-Loop?

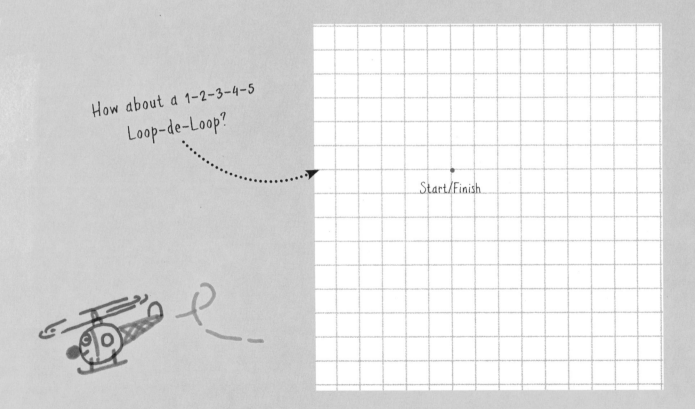

Start/Finish

MAKE YOUR OWN
LOOP-DE-LOOPS HERE!

Golden Spiral

IF YOU LIKE DRAWING SPIRALS, YOU CAN USE A SPECIAL NUMBER PATTERN TO MAKE THE PERFECT SPIRAL! YOU'LL NEED YOUR COMPASS.

1 Draw a 1x1 box.

2 Draw another 1x1 box below.

3 Draw a 2x2 box on the right of the two 1x1 boxes.

4 Above the 2x2 box, draw a 3x3 box.

5 Draw a 5x5 box on the left.

6 Add an 8x8 box below.

7 Draw a 13x13 box on the right.

8 Now, use your compass to draw a curve through each box in turn. Put the compass point on the red dot at the bottom corner of box 1 and sketch a quarter of a circle. Continue the circle through box 2.

9 For box 3, move your compass point to the gray dot and stretch it so the pencil reaches the top right-hand corner. Draw the curve.

10 Follow the color coding for boxes 4 – 7, being sure to move and adjust your compass each time.

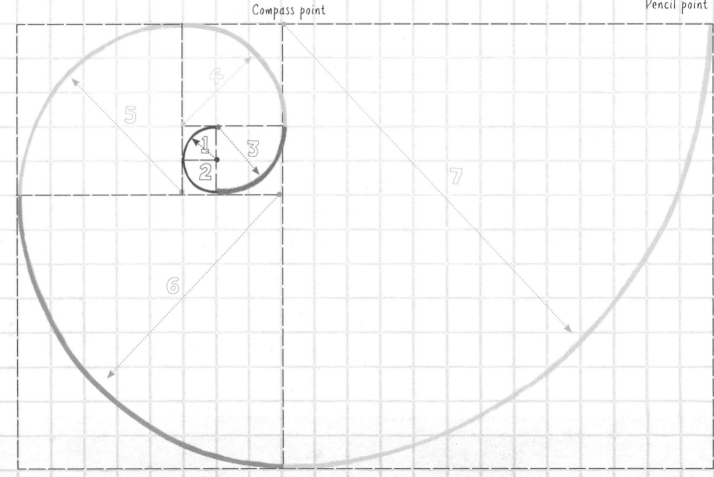

Compass point

Pencil point

EACH BOX CONTAINS ONE
QUARTER OF A CIRCLE.

DRAW YOUR OWN
Golden Spiral HERE:

Squaretangles

HERE'S A PUZZLE THAT'S FUN TO SOLVE-AND ALSO MAKES BEAUTIFUL ART!

BREAK EACH RECTANGLE INTO THE SMALLEST NUMBER OF SQUARES YOU CAN.

Here's a rectangle broken into the least number of squares possible—in this case, three.

TRY THIS ONE!

Can you find six squares?

HAVE FUN COLORING THEM IN!

Can you find eight squares?

THIS PUZZLE IS ALSO FUN WHEN YOU START WITH A SQUARE!

Break this square into the least number of smaller squares.

Use this square.

CHALLENGE

Can you beat ten?

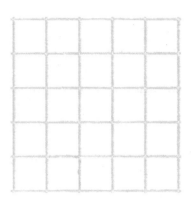

NOW TRY
THIS SQUARE!

Are some sizes of squares and rectangles more interesting than others to fill with smaller squares? Try more, using the graph paper at the back of the book.

Art on a Slant

When you draw a picture, it looks normal when you look at it from the front—everything is in proportion. But what if you tilt the page? Now the image looks funny. When you make anamorphic art, you switch this around. Anamorphic art streeeeetches the picture so that it looks strange when looked at straight on, but everything is in proportion from a new angle.

Look at the pixel art robot below. It looks distorted—all stretched out. Now try tilting the page, holding the eye symbol in the corner just below your eye. Keep tilting the page until it's horizontal and the robot looks like it should, all its proportions correct.
Pretty cool!

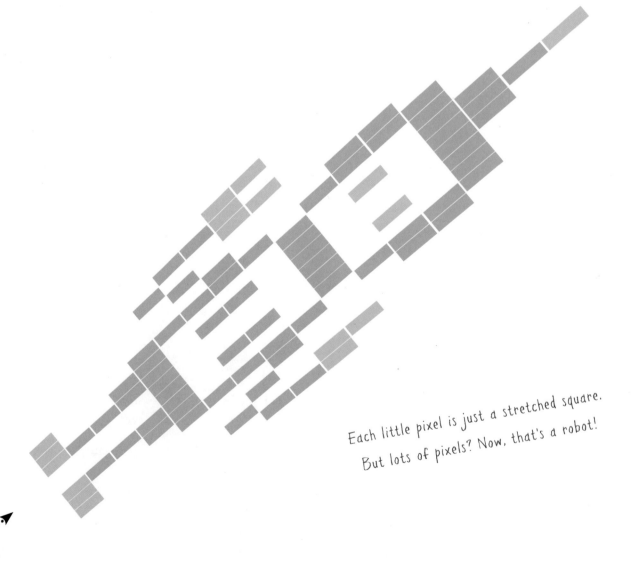

Each little pixel is just a stretched square.
But lots of pixels? Now, that's a robot!

ANAMORPHIC VIEWPOINT. COVER ONE EYE AND HOLD THE PAGE HORIZONTAL TO SEE THE ANAMORPHIC IMAGE

DRAW YOUR OWN

TRY CREATING YOUR OWN ANAMORPHIC PIXEL ART.
DRAW A PIXEL IMAGE IN THE GRID BELOW, THEN COPY
IT ONTO THE DISTORTED GRID ON THE RIGHT. USE THE
AXIS NUMBERS TO HELP YOU COPY EXACTLY!

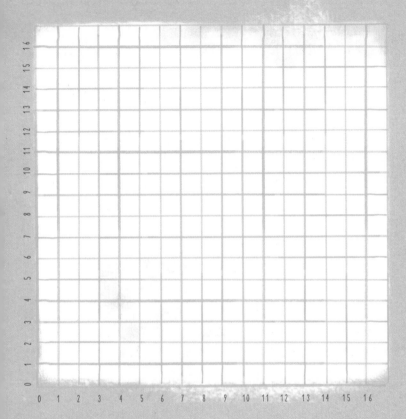

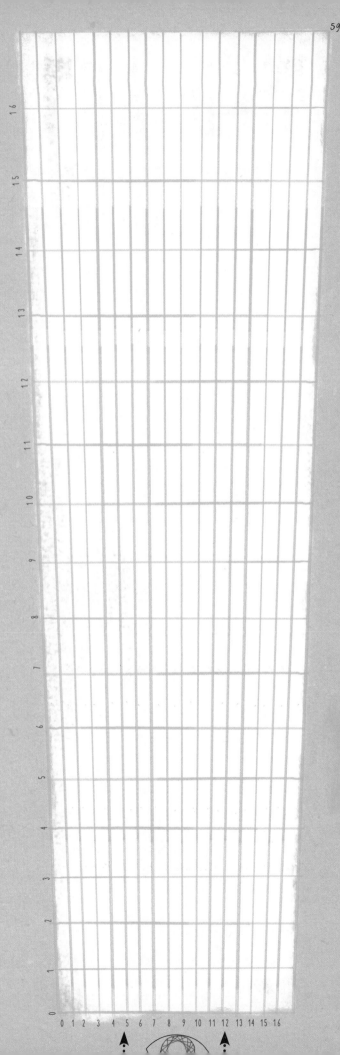

The image on the square grid will look like
it should. When copied, it will look distorted.
Then, when held horizontally, it should look
normal again—like it does on the square grid.

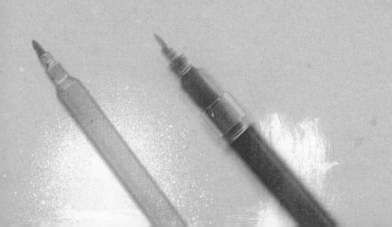

3-D ART

HOW DO YOU DRAW SOMETHING
THAT LOOKS 3-D ON A FLAT PAGE?
USE THE TRICK OF PERSPECTIVE!

1 Draw a line (this is the "horizon").

Add a dot in the center.
This is the "vanishing point."

2 Draw squares on,
above and below
the line.

3 Add lines connecting the corners of
the squares and the vanishing point.

If your square is on top of the
line, like square 1, draw two lines.

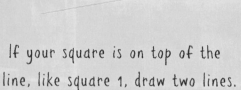

If your square is entirely above or below the
line, like squares 2 and 3, draw three lines.

 NOW TO CREATE THE BOXES...

To make a long box, erase
a little bit of the line.

For a short box, erase
a lot of the line.

Draw vertical and
horizontal lines to
complete each box.

WHOA! FLYING BOXES! ADD SOME MORE!

MAKE YOUR OWN 3-D DRAWING

WHEN YOU LOOK OFF INTO THE DISTANCE, THINGS THAT ARE FARTHER AWAY LOOK SMALLER. LINES THAT ARE ALWAYS THE SAME DISTANCE APART LOOK LIKE THEY MEET. THIS ISN'T REALLY TRUE-THINGS DON'T ACTUALLY SHRINK AS THEY GET FARTHER AWAY.

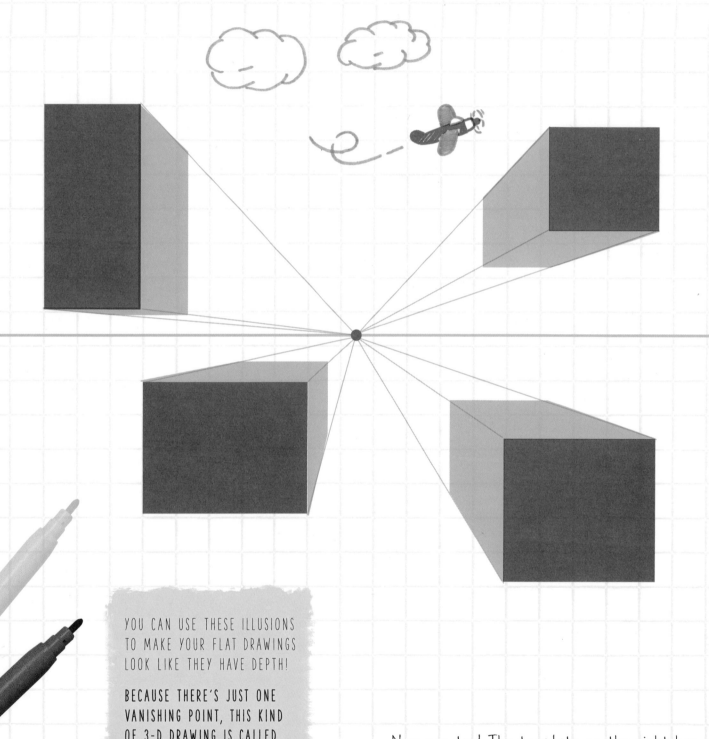

YOU CAN USE THESE ILLUSIONS TO MAKE YOUR FLAT DRAWINGS LOOK LIKE THEY HAVE DEPTH!

BECAUSE THERE'S JUST ONE VANISHING POINT, THIS KIND OF 3-D DRAWING IS CALLED ONE-POINT PERSPECTIVE.

Now you try! The template on the right has a few helpful lines to get you started.

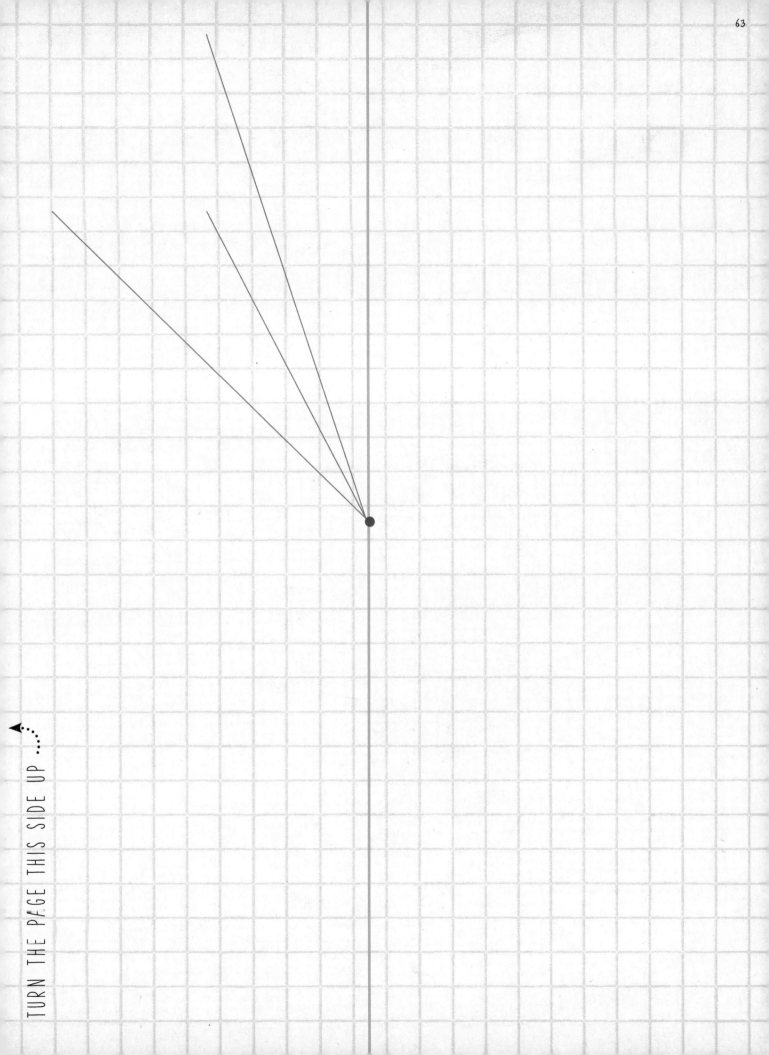

TURN THE PAGE THIS SIDE UP ......

Impossible Triangle

YOU CAN USE THE ILLUSION OF PERSPECTIVE TO DRAW IMPOSSIBLE 3-D SHAPES!

1 Draw a perfect equilateral triangle.

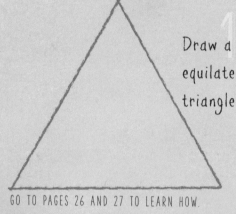

GO TO PAGES 26 AND 27 TO LEARN HOW.

2 Draw a second perfect triangle inside. Extend the edges of the new triangle so they cross and touch the sides of the first.

Connect the ends.

3 Draw a third triangle inside the second, extending the edges as before.

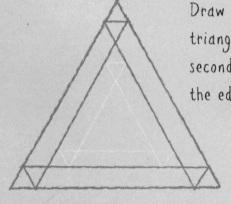

4 Trace an "L" shape on the inside of the first triangle. Then, outline the outer triangle in black marker or pen.

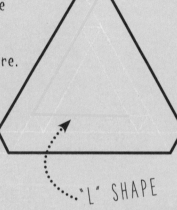

"L" SHAPE

5 Rotate your triangle and repeat Step 4 twice. Now, erase the unwanted lines.

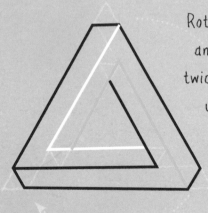

6 ADD A LITTLE SHADING AND YOU ARE DONE!

NOW MAKE YOUR OWN
IMPOSSIBLE TRIANGLES!

Adapt the method to make an
IMPOSSIBLE STAR!

COLORING CONUNDRUM!

Can you color all the empty spaces so that no two spaces that share an edge are the same color?

USE NO MORE THAN
TWO DIFFERENT COLORS.

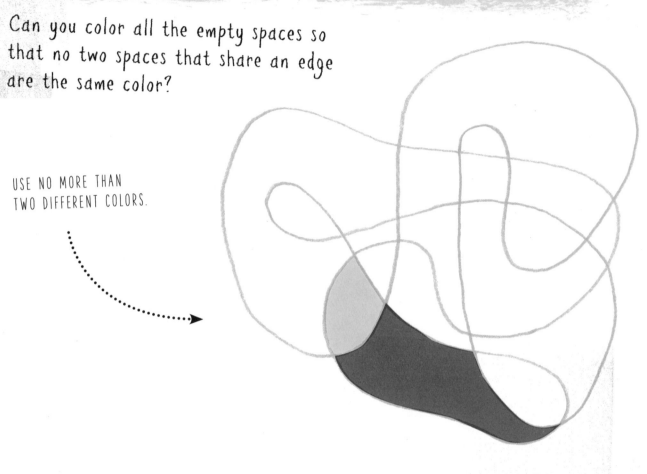

USE NO MORE THAN
FOUR DIFFERENT COLORS.

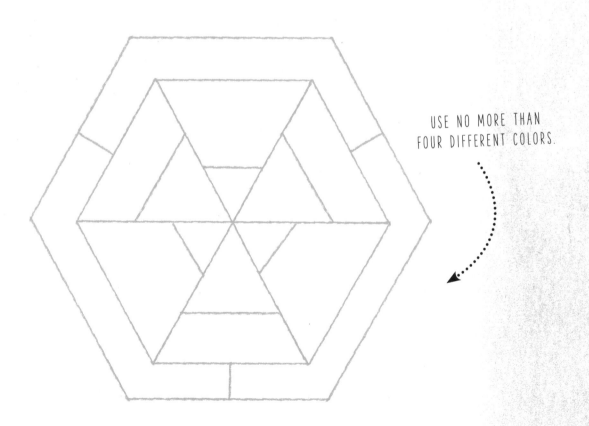

DRAW A SQUIGGLE OR A BUNCH OF OVERLAPPING SHAPES,
AND CREATE YOUR OWN COLOR CRAZY PATTERNS HERE!

MORE COLORING CONUNDRUMS

USE THREE COLORS FOR
THIS CONUNDRUM.
REMEMBER THAT NO TWO
SPACES THAT SHARE
AN EDGE SHOULD
BE THE SAME COLOR!

This shape is all
right angles and
broken lines!
You need four colors.

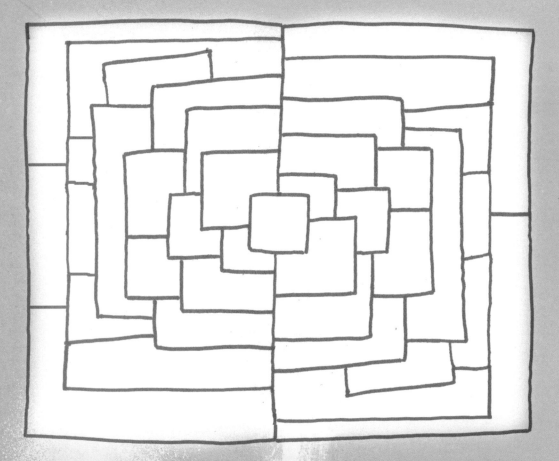

MAKE YOUR OWN COLORING CONUNDRUM HERE!

Can you make up your own coloring conundrum that can't be colored with less than four colors? Try it!

 Did you know that it's impossible to make a coloring conundrum that needs more than four colors to be completely colored?

SUPER STARS

CAN YOU MAKE A SEVEN-POINTED STAR? HOW ABOUT A 25-POINTED STAR? IT'S SIMPLE—ALL YOU NEED TO DO IS COUNT!

SEVEN-POINTED STAR:

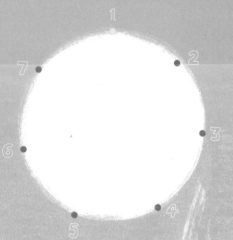

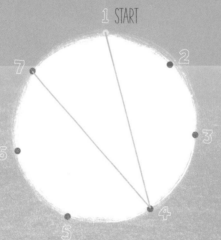

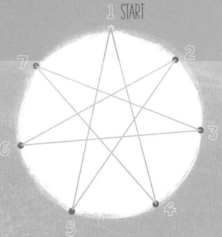

1 Draw seven dots in a circle.

2 Connect every third dot.

3 Keep connecting every third dot until you get back to where you started!

START

TRY THIS! CONNECT EVERY SECOND DOT.

TRY THIS! CONNECT EVERY FOURTH DOT.

SEEING STARS

You don't have to start with seven dots—and you don't have to connect every third! Try starting with nine, eleven or even 30 dots and making your connecting number larger or smaller.

ELEVEN DOTS—CONNECT EVERY THIRD DOT

NINE DOTS—YOU CHOOSE

FIFTEEN DOTS! CONNECT EVERY THIRD OR FOURTH DOT TO MAKE A WIDE STAR

SEVENTEEN DOTS! CONNECT EVERY THIRD OR FOURTH FOR A WIDE STAR, OR EVERY SEVENTH OR EIGHTH FOR A POINTY STAR!

OR EVERY SIXTH OR SEVENTH TO MAKE A POINTY STAR!

EULER'S CHALLENGE

Can you trace over these drawings—starting and
ending at the same dot—without lifting your pencil?
You can only go over each line once!

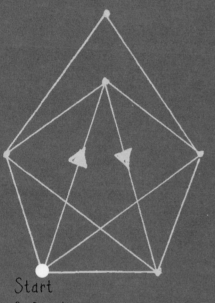

Start
& finish

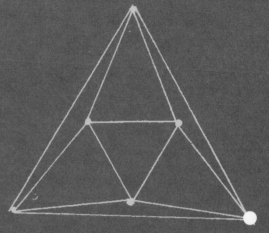

Start & finish

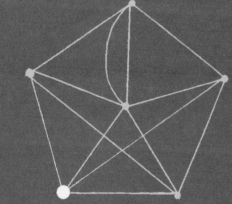

Start & finish

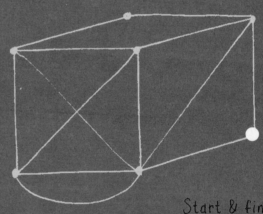

Start
& finish

Start & finish

THIS ONE MIGHT LOOK
TRICKY BUT DO YOU SEE
THE EIGHT-POINTED STAR
IN THE MIDDLE?

IT'S IMPOSSIBLE!

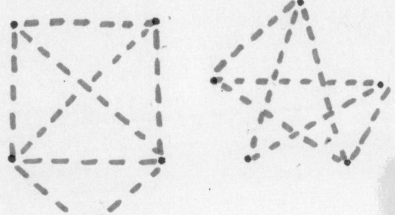

These are both impossible. No matter how many different ways you try, you can't start and end in the same place and trace every line without lifting your pencil. Try it and see!

WHY ARE SOME IMPOSSIBLE?

A LONG TIME AGO, A MATHEMATICIAN NAMED LEONHARD EULER FOUND OUT THAT THIS TRICK WORKS ONLY IF EVERY POINT IN THE DRAWING HAS AN EVEN NUMBER OF LINES COMING OUT OF IT. SOME POINTS IN THESE DRAWINGS HAVE THREE LINES-SO THEY'RE IMPOSSIBLE!

MAKE YOUR OWN EULER CHALLENGES HERE!

TAKE IT FURTHER

Not sure what to do next? Here are some ideas for smart art projects.

IDEAS FOR PROJECTS

Pages 24–27 and 38–39 show you how to draw perfect triangles and hexagons using a compass and a ruler. What other perfect shapes can you draw with just those tools?

When making a Pascal's Triangle (pages 32–33) you don't have to start with a 1 at the top. Try different numbers and ways of combining them.

Make your own Stomachion puzzle (pages 34–37). Cut different shapes out of a square and see what shapes you can make.

Make your Squaretangles drawing (pages 56–57) into a puzzle! Cut out the individual squares and challenge a friend to put them back into a rectangle.

Can you make a transformation tessellation (pages 40–43) that covers a ball? How about a cube? Try tessellating lots of different shapes!

PUT IT TOGETHER

After making your own Squaretangle (pages 56–57), fill the empty squares with infinite circles (pages 20–21) or make them into webs (pages 18–19).

Fill the spaces in your stars from pages 70–71 with patterns to make a beautiful Mandala (pages 22–23).

Try coloring in your other drawings, such as tessellations, circles, squared-rectangles, and much more, using the four-color trick from pages 68–69!

Make a collage of your favorite drawings! Or, start your own math art book and fill it with awesome original creations!

BEYOND DRAWING

Make the parabolic curves from pages 16–19 or the stars from pages 70–71 out of string! Draw a circle with dots or a pair of axes on a piece of paper and glue the paper to a piece of cardboard. Press pins into the dots. Wrap colored string between the pins where you would normally draw lines!

Use colored glue to paint the outline for an Only Four Colors drawing (pages 66–69) on a piece of glass or clear plastic. Fill in the spaces with transparent colored paint (following the four colors rule) to make a stained-glass window!

The Mandalas from pages 22–23 are traditionally made from colored sand. Sketch out your Mandala pattern on a circle of paper and lightly paint it with glue. Carefully sprinkle colored sand or salt to fill in your Mandala!

Make tessellation-shaped cookie cutters! Use heavy-duty aluminum foil or thin plastic to make tessellation puzzle piece cookie cutters (pages 42–43 or 46–47).

Tessellations (pages 42–47) make great decorations for any surface. Got an empty wall? Make some tessellation wallpaper! Need a pattern for a T-shirt? Cover it with a tessellation! You can draw tessellations on mugs, flower pots, bracelets and pillows to make great gifts.

GLOSSARY

ANAMORPHIC ART: distorted artwork that only looks normal when seen from a particular viewpoint or through a special lens.

ANGLE: the space, measured in degrees, between two lines that meet in a single point.

AXIS (plural AXES): a horizontal or vertical line to help place the position of points called coordinates.

CARDIOID: a curve shape that looks like a heart, made up of overlapping circles.

COMPASS: a drawing tool used for making perfect circles.

DEGREE: the unit of measurement used for measuring angles.

DIGIT: a single number from 0 to 9, used in writing a number. For example, 28 has 2 digits: 2 and 8.

EQUILATERAL: a shape whose sides are all the same length.

EULERIAN CURVE: a graph in which you can trace over all of the edges exactly once, starting and stopping at the same point, without lifting your pencil.

EVEN NUMBER: a number that can be divided evenly by 2.

FRACTAL: a shape or pattern that repeats itself forever. Each part is made up of a scaled-down version of the whole shape.

GRAPH: in this book, a drawing made by connecting dots with lines.

GRID: a background covering a flat space made of crossed lines. Grids often consist of squares, but they can be made up of triangles or hexagons, too.

HEPTAGON: a seven-sided shape.

HEXAGON: a six-sided shape.

HORIZON: the line that separates a perspective drawing into two sections.

HORIZONTAL: the word that describes a line that extends from side to side.

INFINITY: something without limit or that never ends.

KOCH SNOWFLAKE: a type of fractal made by dividing the edges of a triangle into smaller and smaller triangles of the same shape.

LINK: two or more circles that are interlocked.

MANDALA: a spiritual symbol in Hinduism and Buddhism, often made from a circle and containing a lot of symmetry.

MULTIPLE (OF): a number is a multiple of a second number if the first can be divided perfectly by the second. For example, 6 is a multiple of 3 because 6 divided by 3 is 2.

OCTAGON: an eight-sided shape.

ODD NUMBER: a number that cannot be divided evenly by 2.

PARABOLIC CURVE: a U-shaped curve that slowly grows wider as it grows taller.

PENTAGON: a five-sided shape.

PERSPECTIVE: the way of drawing 3-D objects on a 2-D (flat) surface so that they appear to have the correct height, width and length.

PROTRACTOR: a tool used for measuring and drawing angles.

RADIUS: the distance between the outside of a circle and its center point.

RECTANGLE: a shape that has four straight sides, whose opposites are equal, and four right angles.

RIGHT TRIANGLE:

a triangle with a 90° angle in one corner.

ROTATION: turning a shape around a point, such as one of its corners.

ROTATION SYMMETRY: an image with rotation symmetry does not change when rotated by a certain amount. A pattern with rotation symmetry is made by repeating a shape in a circle.

SEQUENCE: numbers listed in a particular order.

SIERPINSKI TRIANGLE: a type of fractal made by dividing an equilateral triangle into smaller equilateral triangles. The process is then repeated with the smaller equilateral triangles.

SQUARE: a shape with four sides that are all the same length and angles that are all 90°.

STOMACHION: a puzzle made of fourteen different shapes that fit inside a square.

SYMMETRY: a shape has symmetry if it does not look different when it is moved in a particular way, such as when it is rotated.

TESSELLATION: a repeating, symmetrical pattern of shapes. It has no gaps or overlaps.

TRANSLATION SYMMETRY: an image with translation symmetry does not change when the image is moved or repeated. A pattern with translation symmetry is made by repeating a shape without turning or changing it in any way.

TRIANGLE: a three-sided shape.

VANISHING POINT: the point in a 2-D (flat) drawing of a 3-D space where the perspective lines meet.

VERTICAL: the word that describes a line that extends up and down.

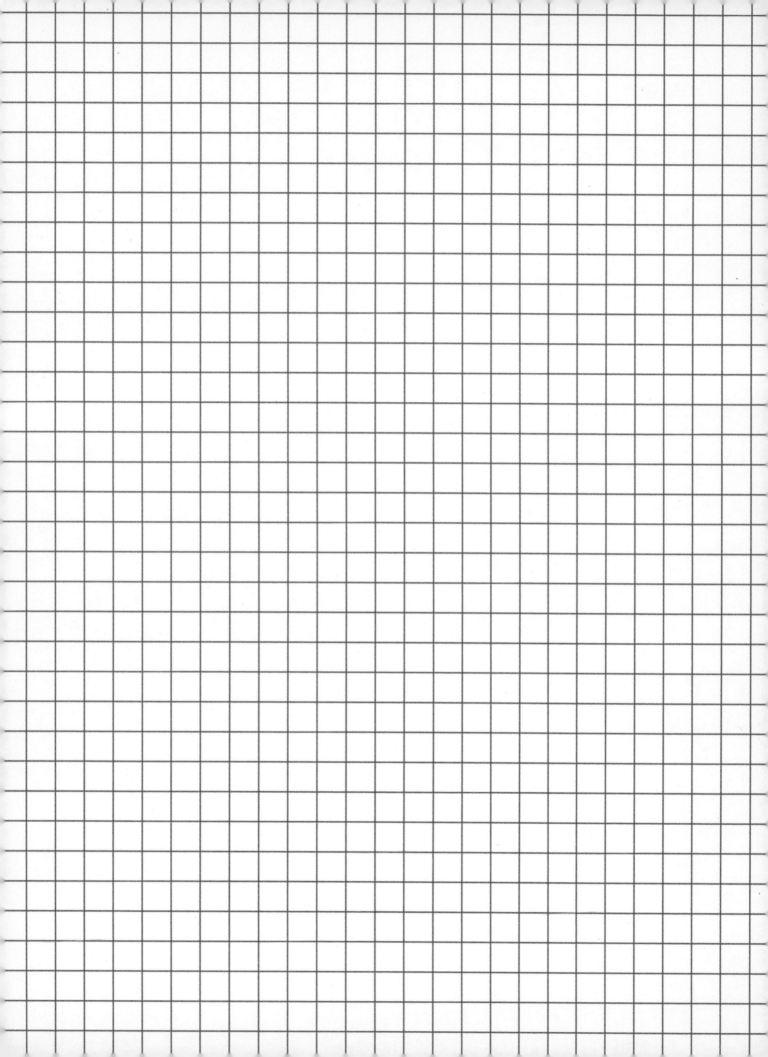